Great River Regional Library
January 2022

THE HAUNTED!

HAUNTED HOUSES AND MANSIONS

A Crabtree Branches Book

THOMAS KINGSLEY TROUPE

School-to-Home Support for Caregivers and Teachers

This high-interest book is designed to motivate striving students with engaging topics while building fluency, vocabulary, and an interest in reading. Here are a few questions and activities to help the reader build upon his or her comprehension skills.

Before Reading:
- *What do I think this book is about?*
- *What do I know about this topic?*
- *What do I want to learn about this topic?*
- *Why am I reading this book?*

During Reading:
- *I wonder why...*
- *I'm curious to know...*
- *How is this like something I already know?*
- *What have I learned so far?*

After Reading:
- *What was the author trying to teach me?*
- *What are some details?*
- *How did the photographs and captions help me understand more?*
- *Read the book again and look for the vocabulary words.*
- *What questions do I still have?*

Extension Activities:
- *What was your favorite part of the book? Write a paragraph on it.*
- *Draw a picture of your favorite thing you learned from the book.*

TABLE OF CONTENTS

Home Scary Home 4
Villisca Murder House 6
Borley Rectory 8
Höfdi House 12
The White House 14
Biltmore Mansion 18
Morgan House, India 20
Raynham Hall 22
Winchester Mystery House 24
Conclusion 28
Glossary 30
Index 31
Websites to Visit 31
About the Author 32

Home Scary Home

The wooden floor creaks and you tiptoe through the darkness. The door behind you slams shut, trapping you inside. Your flashlight flickers and a moment later the house around you is completely dark. The sound of slow footsteps move closer and closer to you.
A child's voice whispers somewhere in the haunted house!

There are places around the world that people believe are haunted. Houses and mansions are where the living live. Unfortunately, some of them might be homes for the dead.

Grab your flashlight and take a deep breath. You're about to discover why these houses and mansions are among...
THE HAUNTED.

FRIGHTENING FACT
Forty-five percent of Americans believe that ghosts and demons exist.

VILLISCA MURDER HOUSE

The small house on the corner in Villisca, Iowa, has a terrible past. In 1912, eight people were murdered there in the middle of the night. The killer was never found.

People believe the house is now haunted by the spirits of the Moore family. Photos taken during tours sometimes reveal strange shadows. At night, people claim to hear children's voices.

BORLEY RECTORY

In Essex, England, haunted house discussions usually include the Borley **Rectory**. The home was built in 1863 over the remains of an old **monastery**.

Many believe the house was haunted by a spirit known as the Lady in White. The ghost is believed to be of a girl who Einar saw die from poisoning.

THE WHITE HOUSE

One of the most well-known houses in the world might be one of the most haunted. The White House in Washington, D.C., is where the President of the United States lives.

Some believe the nation's president isn't the only president roaming the halls. The spirits of past presidents and their families sometimes pay their former home a visit. First Lady Dolley Madison's ghost has been spotted tending the garden.

Dolley Madison

In 1940, Prime Minister Winston Churchill stayed at the White House. After taking a bath, he spotted the ghost of Abraham Lincoln standing by the Lincoln bedroom's fireplace.

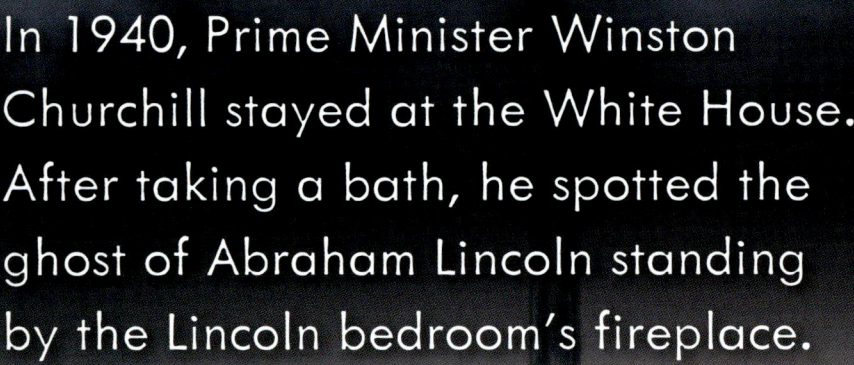

FRIGHTENING FACT

David Burnes sold the land where the White House was built. His ghostly voice is often heard in the Oval Office where the president works.

Ghostly First Lady Abigail Adams could be seen with her arms outstretched in the East Room.

Abigail Adams

17

BILTMORE MANSION

In Asheville, North Carolina, sits the beautiful Biltmore Mansion. The home belonged to George Vanderbilt, who came from a wealthy family.

George died in 1914, but never bothered to leave his mansion. His ghost is often spotted reading in his **massive** library. Some visitors have heard laughter and the sounds of a phantom dinner party.

George Vanderbilt

The mansion is the largest house in the United States at 175,000 square feet (16,258 square meters) with 250 rooms inside.

Morgan House, India

The Morgan House was a mansion in Kalimpong, India, that overlooked the Kachenjunga mountain range. It seemed like a peaceful place for the newly married Morgans to live their lives.

The place is anything but peaceful. Mrs. Morgan died suddenly under mysterious circumstances. Recent visitors sometimes hear the sounds of high-heeled shoes walking the halls.

FRIGHTENING FACT

After the Morgan House was abandoned, it was converted into a hotel. Many famous Bollywood movie actors have stayed there.

Raynham Hall

In Norfolk, England, Raynham Hall's most famous spooky resident is a ghost known as the Brown Lady. She earned the nickname for the brown **brocade** dress she wore.

A photo taken in 1936 showed the ghost walking down the stairs. People who have seen the ghost claim there are black holes where her eyes should be!

According to legend, the "Brown Lady of Raynham Hall" is the ghost of Lady Dorothy Walpole.

Winchester Mystery House

Sarah Winchester was an **heiress** to the Winchester gun fortune. After her baby daughter and husband died, she moved to San Jose, California. There she bought an eight room farmhouse.

Sarah Winchester

In 1886, she had workers add on to her new home. It was one of the longest renovations, stopping when she died in 1922.

FRIGHTENING FACT

A *medium* told Sarah she needed to change the house and to keep working on it or she would die. The construction lasted for 38 years.

The house became one of the strangest mansions ever built. There are stairways and doors that lead nowhere. Hidden passages and secret rooms are everywhere. Sarah even had a séance room built to communicate with the dead.

Visitors to the Winchester Mystery House claim to see a ghostly maintenance worker. Others have had their clothes tugged at by invisible hands.

The strange design of the house was meant to appease the spirits living there. Sarah believed it was haunted by the ghosts of people killed by Winchester firearms.

CONCLUSION

No one knows for sure if ghosts truly haunt houses and mansions. What one person sees, another might explain away.

It's up to you to decide for yourself.
If you hear or see something creepy,
write it down or capture it with a camera.
The evidence you discover might bring us
closer to understanding...THE HAUNTED.

GLOSSARY

appease (uh-PEEZ): To help make calmer

brocade (broh-KAYD): Cloth with a raised design on it

gazebo (guh-ZEE-boh): A small open-sided building in a garden or park

heiress (AIR-uhss): A woman who is given money or property after another person's death

massive (MASS-iv): Very large, heavy

medium (MEE-dee-uhm): A person who communicates messages from the dead to the living

monastery (MON-uh-ster-ee): A place where people live and worship

rectory (REK-tor-ee): The house where a pastor of a church lives

séance (SAY-ahnss): A meeting where people try to communicate with spirits

INDEX

Adams, Abigail 17
Churchill, Winston 16
ghost(s) 5, 10, 11, 13, 15, 16, 17, 19, 22, 23, 27, 28
Lincoln, Abraham 16
mansion(s) 5, 18, 19, 20, 26, 28
nun 9, 10
poisoning 13
séance 11, 26
secret rooms 26
spirits 7, 11, 13, 15, 27
Villisca Murder House 6, 7
White House 14-17
Winchester, Sarah 24, 25, 26, 27

WEBSITES TO VISIT

https://kids.kiddle.co/Ghost

www.hauntedrooms.co.uk/ghost-stories-kids-scary-childrens

www.ghostsandgravestones.com/how-to-ghost-hunt

ABOUT THE AUTHOR

Thomas Kingsley Troupe

Thomas Kingsley Troupe is the author of a whole pile of books for kids. He's written about ghosts, Bigfoot, werewolves, and even a book about dirt. When he's not writing or reading, he investigates the paranormal as part of the Twin Cities Paranormal Society. He lives in Woodbury, Minnesota with his 2 sons.

Produced by: Blue Door Education for Crabtree Publishing
Written by: Thomas Kingsley Troupe
Designed by: Jennifer Dydyk
Edited by: Kelli Hicks
Proofreader: Crystal Sikkens

The images/photos depicting "ghosts" in this book are artists' interpretations. The publisher does not claim these are actual images/photos taken of the ghosts mentioned in this book.

Cover: © Netfalls Remy Musser, skull on cover and throughout book ©Fer Gregory, pages 4-5 creepy picture borders here and throughout book © Dmitry Natashin, page 4 © Victoria Denisova, page 5 house © jordanlieberman, messy floor © phoelixDE, page 6 © zef art, page 9 © Sergey Novikov, page 10 © LightField Studios, page 12 © danneuf, page 13 © Lario Tus, page 14 © BrianPlrwin, page 15 Dolley Madison, page 16 Abraham Lincoln, page 17 Abigail Adams © Everett Collection, page 18 © Konstantin L, page 21 © zefart, page 23 stairs © fl1photo, "ghost" © Slava Gerj, pages 24-25 and page 26 (top) Winchester Mystery House © Dragan Jovanovic, page 26 (bottom) © CREATISTA, page 27 bedroom © lv-olga , hand © IDmutroll, page 28 © Lukiyanova Natalia frenta, page 29 © Michael D Edwards. All images from Shutterstock.com except page 7 courtesy of the Library of Congress, page 15 garden © courtesy of the Library of Congress, pages 16 and 17 Whitehouse rooms courtesy of the Library of Congress, page 20 image released into public domain by Subhrajyoti07, Page 22 Raynham Hall © Nigel Jones https://creativecommons.org/licenses/by-sa/2.0/ background Sketch by John Sell Cotman public domain image, page 24 Sarah Winchester public domain photograph taken in 1865 by the Taber Photographic Company of San Francisco

Library and Archives Canada Cataloguing in Publication

Title: Haunted houses and mansions / Thomas Kingsley Troupe.
Names: Troupe, Thomas Kingsley, author.
Description: Series statement: The haunted! | "A Crabtree branches book". | Includes index. | Includes bibliographical references and index.
Identifiers: Canadiana (print) 20210220260 |
  Canadiana (ebook) 20210220279 |
  ISBN 9781427155573 (hardcover) |
  ISBN 9781427155634 (softcover) |
  ISBN 9781427155696 (HTML) |
  ISBN 9781427155757 (EPUB) |
  ISBN 9781427155818 (read-along ebook)
Subjects: LCSH: Haunted houses—Juvenile literature. | LCSH: Ghosts—Juvenile literature.
Classification: LCC BF1475 .T76 2022 | DDC j133.1/22—dc23

Library of Congress Cataloging-in-Publication Data

Names: Troupe, Thomas Kingsley, author.
Title: Haunted houses and mansions / Thomas Kingsley Troupe.
Description: New York, NY : Crabtree Publishing Company, [2022] | Series: The haunted! - a Crabtree Branches book | Includes index.
Identifiers: LCCN 2021022570 (print) |
  LCCN 2021022571 (ebook) |
  ISBN 9781427155573 (hardcover) |
  ISBN 9781427155634 (paperback) |
  ISBN 9781427155696 (ebook) |
  ISBN 9781427155757 (epub) |
  ISBN 9781427155818
Subjects: LCSH: Haunted houses--Juvenile literature. | Ghosts--Juvenile literature.
Classification: LCC BF1475 .T76 2022 (print) | LCC BF1475 (ebook) | DDC 133.1/22--dc23
LC record available at https://lccn.loc.gov/2021022570
LC ebook record available at https://lccn.loc.gov/2021022571

Crabtree Publishing Company
www.crabtreebooks.com   1-800-387-7650

Printed in the U.S.A./072021/CG20210514

Copyright © 2022 **CRABTREE PUBLISHING COMPANY**

All rights reserved. No part of this publication may be reproduced, stored in a retrieval system or be transmitted in any form or by any means, electronic, mechanical, photocopying, recording, or otherwise, without the prior written permission of Crabtree Publishing Company. In Canada: We acknowledge the financial support of the Government of Canada through the Canada Book Fund for our publishing activities.

Published in the United States
Crabtree Publishing
347 Fifth Avenue, Suite 1402-145
New York, NY, 10016

Published in Canada
Crabtree Publishing
616 Welland Ave.
St. Catharines, ON, L2M 5V6